Burns and Lambert

The Rosary of the Blessed Virgin Mary

With Prayers and Points of Meditation

Burns and Lambert

The Rosary of the Blessed Virgin Mary
With Prayers and Points of Meditation

ISBN/EAN: 9783337274962

Printed in Europe, USA, Canada, Australia, Japan

Cover: Foto ©Lupo / pixelio.de

More available books at **www.hansebooks.com**

THE

ROSARY

OF

𝕿𝖍𝖊 𝕭𝖑𝖊𝖘𝖘𝖊𝖉 𝖁𝖎𝖗𝖌𝖎𝖓 𝕸𝖆𝖗𝖞;

WITH

PRAYERS AND POINTS OF MEDITATION.

ADAPTED FOR THE USE OF

MEMBERS OF THE LIVING ROSARY.

LONDON:

BURNS & LAMBERT, 17 PORTMAN STREET,

AND 63 PATERNOSTER ROW.

POINTS OF MEDITATION.

The Angelical Salutation.

---

1. The most Holy Trinity consents to the Incarnation of Jesus Christ.

2. Mary is chosen to be the Mother of the Incarnate Word.

3. The Angel Gabriel announces that happiness to Mary.

4. Mary prays in her holy solitude.

5. The Angel salutes her, saying, " Hail Mary, full of grace, the Lord is with thee."

6. Mary is troubled at the sight and speech of the Angel.

7. The Angel says, " Fear not, Mary, thou shalt conceive by the power of the Holy Ghost."

8. Mary answers, " Behold the handmaid of the Lord, be it done unto me according to thy word."

9. The Holy Ghost overshadows her.

10. And the Word was made Flesh, and dwelt among us.

Ejaculation.

Jesus, whom thou didst conceive, remaining ever Virgin.

Let us contemplate, in this mystery, how the angel Gabriel saluted our Blessed Lady with the title, "Full of Grace," and declared unto her the Incarnation of our Lord and Saviour Jesus Christ.

1 Pater, 10 Aves, 1 Gloria.

Let us pray.

O Holy Mary, Queen of Virgins; through the most high mystery of the Incarnation of thy beloved Son, our Lord Jesus Christ, wherein our salvation was begun, obtain for us, through thy most holy intercession, light to understand the greatness of the benefit He hath bestowed upon us, in vouchsafing to become our Brother, and giving thee, His own beloved Mother, to be our Mother also. Amen.

Virtue—HUMILITY.

The Visitation.

1. Mary, with great humility and charity, goes to visit her cousin St. Elisabeth.
2. Mary guided by the Holy Ghost, and accompanied by the holy angels.
3. Mary crosses the mountains in haste.
4. Mary is received with great joy by her cousin, St. Elisabeth.
5. St. John is sanctified in his mother's womb.
6. St. Elisabeth says, " Blessed is the Fruit of thy womb."
7. Mary replies, " My soul doth magnify the Lord."
8. Elisabeth exclaims, " Whence is this to me, that the Mother of my Lord should come to visit me ?"
9. The house of Zacharias supremely blessed by the visits of Jesus and Mary.
10. Mary serves her cousin in all humble offices for the space of three months.

Ejaculation.

Jesus, whom thou didst bear with thee to visit St. Elisabeth.

LET us contemplate, in this mystery, how the Blessed Virgin Mary, understanding from the angel that her cousin Saint Elisabeth had conceived, went with haste into the mountains of Judea to visit her, bearing her Divine Son within her womb, and remained with her three months.

1 Pater, 10 Aves, 1 Gloria.

Let us pray.

O Holy Virgin, most spotless mirror of humility; by that exceeding charity which moved thee to visit thy holy cousin Saint Elisabeth, obtain for us, through thine intercession, that our hearts being visited by thy Divine Son, and freed from all sin, we may praise and give thanks to Him for ever. Amen.

Virtue—CHARITY.

PATRON

POINTS OF MEDITATION.

The Birth of Jesus Christ.

---

1. Mary gives birth to a Child, and remains a Virgin.
2. Mary gives birth to Jesus, and wraps Him in swaddling clothes.
3. Mary contemplates Jesus with love and astonishment.
4. Mary embraces Jesus, and presses Him to her heart.
5. Mary feeds Jesus with her Virginal milk.
6. Mary lays Jesus in a manger that Joseph had prepared.
7. Jesus lies in a manger between an ox and an ass.
8. The angels sing, " Glory to God in the highest, on earth peace to men of good will."
9. The shepherds come to visit the Child Jesus.
10. The Magi come to adore the Holy Child, and offer Him presents.

Ejaculation.

Jesus, whom thou didst bring forth, remaining ever Virgin.

LET us contemplate, in this mystery, how the Blessed Virgin Mary, when the time of her delivery was come, brought forth our Redeemer, Jesus Christ, at midnight, and laid Him in a manger, because there was no room for Him in the inns at Bethlehem.

1 Pater, 10 Aves, 1 Gloria.

Let us pray.

O most pure Mother of God; through thy Virginal and most joyful delivery, whereby thou gavest to the world thy only Son, our Saviour, we beseech thee obtain for us, through thine intercession, the grace to lead such pure and holy lives in this world, that we may become worthy to sing, without ceasing, the mercies of thy Son, and His benefits to us, by thee. Amen.

Virtue—POVERTY.

PATRON

POINTS OF MEDITATION.

The Presentation.

---

1. Mary goes to the Temple to offer her Holy Child.

2. Jesus and Mary submit to the law.

3. The way from Nazareth to Jerusalem is long and difficult.

4. Mary carries the Child Jesus in her arms.

5. Mary continues her journey, pondering all these things in her heart.

6. Mary offers Jesus in the Temple.

7. Mary redeems Jesus at the ransom appointed for the poor.

8. Anna rejoices to see her prophecy fulfilled.

9. The holy old man, Simeon, embraces Jesus with joy.

10. Simeon says, " Lord, now lettest Thou Thy servant depart in peace."

Ejaculation.

Jesus, presented by thee in the Temple.

LET us contemplate, in this mystery, how the Blessed Virgin Mary, on the day of her purification, presented the Child Jesus in the Temple, where holy Simeon, giving thanks to God, with great devotion received Him into his arms.

1 Pater, 10 Aves, 1 Gloria.

Let us pray.

O Holy Virgin, most admirable mistress and pattern of obedience, who didst present the Lord of the Temple in the Temple of God ; obtain for us, of thy Blessed Son, that, with holy Simeon and devout Anna, we may praise and glorify Him for ever. Amen.

Virtue—OBEDIENCE TO FAITH.

PATRON _____

POINTS OF MEDITATION.

Mary finds Jesus in the Temple.

---

1. Mary has lost her Beloved Child.
2. Mary deprived of her only Treasure.
3. Mary seeks Him with anxiety.
4. Mary seeks Jesus in the streets and roads.
5. Mary finds Jesus again after three days.
6. Mary finds Jesus in the Temple.
7. Jesus, twelve years old, teaches the doctors.
8. Mary says, " Son, why hast Thou made us sorrowful?"
9. Jesus returns with Mary and Joseph, and is obedient unto them.
10. Mary preserves in her heart the sayings of Jesus.

Ejaculation.
JESUS, whom thou didst find in the Temple.

LET us contemplate, in this mystery, how the Blessed Virgin Mary, after having lost (through no fault of hers) her beloved Son in Jerusalem, sought Him for the space of three days; and at length found Him in the Temple, sitting in the midst of the doctors, hearing them, and asking them questions, being of the age of twelve years.

1 Pater, 10 Aves, 1 Gloria.

Let us pray.

O most Blessed Virgin, more than Martyr in thy sufferings, and yet the comfort of such as are afflicted; by that unspeakable joy, wherewith thy soul was filled, when at length thou didst find thy well-beloved Son in the Temple, teaching in the midst of the doctors; obtain of Him that we may so seek Him and find Him in His Holy Catholic Church, as never more to be separated from Him. Amen.

"Salve Regina," with ℣. and ℟., and Prayers (see end).

Virtue—DESIRE OF BEING UNITED WITH GOD.

PATRON _____

The Prayer and Bloody Sweat of our Blessed Saviour in the Garden.

---

1. Jesus goes into the Garden of Olives.
2. Jesus prays, lying prostrate on the ground.
3. Jesus perseveres in His prayer.
4. Jesus is sorrowful, even unto death.
5. Jesus is bathed in a Sweat of Blood.
6. Jesus submits His will to His Heavenly Father.
7. Jesus warns His disciples to watch and pray.
8. Jesus betrayed by Judas.
9. Jesus is seized by His own creatures.
10. Jesus cruelly bound, and dragged from one judge to another.

Ejaculation.

JESUS, who was agonised for us.

1st Sorrowful Mystery.—The Agony in the Garden.

LET us contemplate, in this mystery, how our Lord Jesus was so afflicted for us in the garden of Gethsemane, that His Body was bathed in a Bloody Sweat, which ran down in great drops to the ground.

1 Pater, 10 Aves, 1 Gloria.

Let us pray.

O most holy Virgin, more than Martyr; by that ardent prayer which our beloved Saviour poured forth to His Heavenly Father in the garden, vouchsafe to intercede for us, that, our passions being reduced to the obedience of reason, we may always, and in all things, conform and subject ourselves to the holy will of God. Amen.

Virtue—FIDELITY TO PRAYER.

PATRON _____

The Scourging of Jesus Christ.

---

1. Jesus is delivered to be scourged.
2. Jesus is falsely accused.
3. Jesus is stripped of his clothes.
4. Jesus is naked in the hands of His executioners.
5. Jesus is fastened to a pillar.
6. Jesus is lashed with scourges.
7. Jesus is bruised with clubs.
8. The Flesh of Jesus is torn with points of lead.
9. The Blood of Jesus flows down to the ground.
10. They unfasten Jesus; He clothes Himself again.

Ejaculation.

JESUS, scourged for our sins.

Let us contemplate, in this mystery, how our Lord Jesus Christ was most cruelly scourged in Pilate's house, the number of stripes they gave Him being about five thousand.

1 Pater, 10 Aves, 1 Gloria.

Let us pray.

O Mother of God, overflowing fountain of patience ; through those stripes thy only and much-beloved Son vouchsafed to suffer for us, obtain of Him for us grace to mortify our rebellious senses, to avoid the occasion of sin, and to be ready to suffer every thing rather than offend God. Amen.

Virtue—SPIRIT OF PENANCE.

POINTS OF MEDITATION.

The Crowning with Thorns.

———

1. Jesus brought forth to be crowned with thorns.
2. They prepare a crown of thorns for Jesus.
3. They force the crown of thorns upon the Head of Jesus.
4. The Head of Jesus is pierced on every side.
5. The Blood flows from the Head of Jesus.
6. The Forehead of Jesus is covered with Blood.
7. The Eyes of Jesus are bathed in Tears.
8. The Lips of Jesus are pale as death.
9. Jesus is clothed in a purple garment, through derision.
10. Jesus is cruelly mocked and derided: " Behold the Man !"

Ejaculation.

Jesus, crowned for us with thorns.

3d Sorrowful Mystery.—The Crowning with Thorns.

LET us contemplate, in this mystery, how those cruel ministers of Satan platted a crown of sharp thorns, and cruelly pressed it on the Sacred Head of our Lord Jesus Christ. .

1 Pater, 10 Aves, 1 Gloria.

Let us pray.

O Mother of our Eternal Prince, the King of Glory; by those sharp thorns wherewith His Sacred Head was pierced, we beseech thee obtain, through thy intercession, that we may be delivered from all motions of pride, and escape that shame which our sins deserve at the day of judgment. Amen.

Virtue—LOVE OF HUMILIATION.

PATRON _____

Jesus carrying His Cross.

---

1. Jesus condemned to be crucified.
2. Jesus lovingly embraces His cross.
3. Jesus carries His cross on His torn and wounded Shoulders.
4. Jesus falls under the weight of His cross for our sins.
5. Jesus, again loaded with His cross, meets His sorrowful Mother.
6. Jesus leaves the impression of His Sacred Countenance on the veil of St. Veronica.
7. Jesus says, " If these things are done in the green wood, what shall be done in the dry ?"
8. None can be found willing to carry the cross for Jesus.
9. Jesus, loaded with His cross, falls at the foot of Calvary.
10. Jesus, again loaded with His cross, ascends the hill of Calvary.

Ejaculation.

Jesus, who didst bear the cross for us.

LET us contemplate, in this mystery, how our Lord Jesus Christ, being sentenced to die, bore, with the most amazing patience, the Cross which was laid upon Him for His greater torment and ignominy.

1 Pater, 10 Aves, 1 Gloria.

Let us pray.

O Holy Virgin, example of patience; by the most painful carrying of the Cross, in which thy Son, our Lord Jesus Christ, bore the heavy weight of our sins, obtain for us of Him, through thine intercession, courage and strength to follow His steps, and bear our cross after Him to the end of our lives. Amen.

Virtue—GOOD USE OF SUFFERINGS.

POINTS OF MEDITATION.

Jesus Crucified.

----

1. Jesus is cruelly stretched upon the cross.
2. His sacred Hands and Feet are pierced through with nails.
3. Jesus is raised upon the cross, and His Blood flows in streams from all His Wounds.
4. Jesus prays for His enemies.
5. Jesus promises Paradise to the penitent thief.
6. Jesus recommends St. John to His holy Mother.
7. Jesus in His thirst is offered vinegar and gall.
8. Jesus cries out, " My God, my God, why hast Thou forsaken Me?"
9. Jesus says, " It is finished !"
10. Jesus gives up His Spirit into the hands of God His Father.

Ejaculation.

Jesus, who died for us upon the cross.

LET us contemplate, in this mystery, how our Lord Jesus Christ, being come to Mount Calvary, was stripped of His clothes, and His Hands and Feet nailed to the Cross, in the presence of His most afflicted Mother.

1 Pater, 10 Aves, 1 Gloria.

Let us pray.

O Holy Mary, Mother of God; as the Body of thy beloved Son was for us stretched upon the Cross, so may we offer up our souls and bodies to be crucified with Him, and our hearts to be pierced with grief at His most bitter Passion ; and thou, O most sorrowful Mother, graciously vouchsafe to help us, by thy all-powerful intercession, to accomplish the work of our salvation. Amen. " Salve Regina," &c.

Virtue—PARDONING OF CRIMES.

PATRON _____

POINTS OF MEDITATION.

The Resurrection of Jesus Christ.

----

1. Jesus rises again the third day from the dead.
2. Jesus conquers death and hell.
3. Jesus consoles and delivers the Holy Fathers.
4. Jesus rises gloriously.
5. Jesus rejoices His Holy Mother.
6. Jesus appears to Mary Magdalene.
7. Jesus appears to Peter, and blesses him.
8. The disciples at Emmaus say, " Did not our hearts burn within us, when He spoke to us?"
9. Jesus appears in the midst of His disciples, and gives them His Peace.
10. Jesus shows His Wounds to St. Thomas.

Ejaculation.

JESUS, who rose again for us from the dead.

Let us contemplate, in this mystery, how our Lord Jesus Christ, triumphing gloriously over death, rose again the third day, immortal and impassible.

1 Pater, 10 Aves, 1 Gloria.

Let us pray.

O glorious Virgin Mary; by that unspeakable joy thou didst receive in the resurrection of thy Divine Son, we beseech thee obtain for us of Him, that our hearts may never go astray after the false joys of this world, but may be for ever wholly employed in the pursuit of the only true and solid joys of heaven. Amen.

Virtue—LIVELY FAITH.

POINTS OF MEDITATION.

The Ascension of Jesus Christ.

---

1. The ascension of Jesus Christ.
2. Jesus ascends into Heaven, by virtue of His own power.
3. Jesus quits His beloved disciples.
4. Jesus promises to remain with them for ever.
5. Jesus promises them the Holy Ghost.
6. As Jesus ascends, He blesses His disciples.
7. Jesus opens Heaven to us.
8. Jesus is seated at the right hand of God His Father.
9. Jesus displays His Five Wounds, on our behalf, to His Heavenly Father.
10. Jesus is our Mediator in Heaven.

Ejaculation.

Jesus, who didst ascend with triumph into Heaven.

LET us contemplate, in this mystery, how our Lord Jesus Christ, forty days after His resurrection, ascended into heaven, attended by angels, in the sight, and to the great admiration, of His most holy Mother and His holy Apostles and disciples.

1 Pater, 10 Aves, 1 Gloria.

Let us pray.

O Mother of God, comforter of the afflicted ; as thy beloved Son, when He ascended into heaven, lifted up His Hands and blessed His Apostles, as He was parted from them ; so vouchsafe, most holy Mother, to lift up thy pure hands to Him on our behalf, that we may enjoy the benefits of His blessing, and of thine, here on earth, and hereafter in heaven. Amen.

Virtue—CHRISTIAN HOPE.

POINTS OF MEDITATION.

The Holy Ghost descends upon the Blessed Virgin and the Apostles.

1. Jesus sends the Holy Ghost.
2. Jesus sends the Comforter.
3. Jesus sends fire upon the earth.
4. The Holy Ghost inflames all hearts with His love.
5. The Holy Ghost enlightens their minds.
6. The Holy Ghost strengthens their hearts.
7. The Holy Ghost gives the gift of tongues.
8. The Holy Ghost distributes His gifts.
9. Come, O Holy Ghost, and visit the hearts of Thy faithful.
10. Come, Holy Ghost, enlighten our hearts with the fire of Thy divine love.

Ejaculation.

Jesus, who didst send down the Holy Ghost upon the Church.

LET us contemplate, in this mystery, how the Lord Jesus Christ, being seated on the right hand of God, sent, as He had promised, the Holy Ghost upon His Apostles, who, after He was ascended, returning to Jerusalem, continued in prayer and supplication with the Blessed Virgin Mary, expecting the performance of His promise.

1 Pater, 10 Aves, 1 Gloria.

Let us pray.

O sacred Virgin, Tabernacle of the Holy Ghost; we beseech thee obtain, by thine intercession, that this most sweet Comforter, whom thy beloved Son sent down upon His Apostles, filling them thereby with spiritual joy, may teach us in this world the true way of salvation, and make us to walk in the way of virtue and good works. Amen.

Virtue—ZEAL FOR SAVING SOULS.

POINTS OF MEDITATION.

The Assumption of the Blessed Virgin.

1. Mary is assumed into Heaven.
2. God the Father receives His well-beloved Daughter.
3. Jesus receives His Holy Mother.
4. The Holy Ghost receives His beloved Spouse.
5. The Seraphims salute Mary.
6. The Angels serve Mary.
7. Mary rejoices all the Heavens.
8. Mary is seated at the right hand of Jesus.
9. Mary is our advocate in Heaven.
10. Mary is our mother and mediatrix in Heaven.

Ejaculation.

JESUS, who hath called thee to Himself.

LET us contemplate, in this mystery, how the glorious Virgin, twelve years after the resurrection of her Son, passed out of this world unto Him, and was by Him assumed into heaven, accompanied by the holy angels.

1 Pater, 10 Aves, 1 Gloria.

Let us pray.

O most prudent Virgin, who, entering the heavenly palaces, didst fill the angels with joy, and man with hope ; vouchsafe to intercede for us at the hour of our death, that, being delivered from the illusions and temptations of the devil, we may joyfully and securely pass out of this temporal state, to enjoy the happiness of eternal life.   Amen.

Virtue—UNION WITH GOD.

POINTS OF MEDITATION.

The Crowning of the Blessed Virgin Mary.

___

1. Mary gloriously crowned in Heaven.
2. Mary crowned through her seraphic love.
3. Mary crowned through her angelical purity.
4. Mary crowned through her profound humility.
5. Mary crowned through her perfect obedience.
6. Mary crowned through her holy prudence.
7. Mary crowned through her admirable patience.
8. Mary crowned through her ardent gratitude.
9. Mary crowned through her holy perseverance.
10. Mary crowned in Heaven, above all Saints and Angels, with the honour due to the Mother of God.

Ejaculation.

JESUS, who hath crowned thee in the Heavens.

LET us contemplate, in this mystery, how the glorious Virgin Mary was, to the great jubilee and exultation of the whole court of Heaven, and particular glory of all the Saints, crowned by her Son with the brightest diadem of glory.

1 Pater, 10 Aves, 1 Gloria.

Let us pray.

O glorious Queen of all the heavenly host ; we beseech thee accept this Rosary, which, as a crown of roses, we offer at thy feet; and grant, most gracious Lady, that, by thy intercession, our souls may be inflamed with so ardent a desire of seeing thee so gloriously crowned, that it may never die within us, until it shall be changed into the happy fruition of thy blessed sight. Amen. " Salve Regina," &c.

Virtue—CONFIDENCE IN MARY.

HAIL, holy Queen, Mother of mercy ;
Our life, our sweetness, and our hope, all hail.
To thee we cry, poor banished sons of Eve ;
To thee we sigh, weeping and mourning in this
vale of tears.
Therefore, O our Advocate,
Turn thou on us those merciful eyes of thine ;
And after this our exile, show us
Jesus, the blessed fruit of thy womb,
O merciful, O kind, O sweet Virgin Mary.

℣. Pray for us, O holy Mother of God.
℟. That we may be made worthy of the promises
of Christ.

Hear, O merciful God, the prayer of thy ser-
vants ; that we who meet together in the society of
the most holy Rosary of the Blessed Virgin, Mother of God, may, through her intercession, be delivered by Thee from the dangers that continually
hang over us ; through the merits of our Lord and
Saviour Jesus Christ. Amen.

O God, whose only-begotten Son, by His life,
death, and resurrection, hath laid open to us the
rewards of everlasting life ; grant, we beseech thee,
that, pondering in our hearts these mysteries in the
most holy Rosary of the Blessed Virgin Mary, we
may imitate what they set forth, and obtain what
they promise ; through the same our Lord and Saviour Jesus Christ. Amen.

www.ingramcontent.com/pod-product-compliance
Lightning Source LLC
Chambersburg PA
CBHW021458090426
42739CB00009B/1773